MY FIRST BILINGUAL ARABIC ENGLISH PICTURE BOOK

500 WORDS OF THE ARABIC LANGUAGE
A VISUAL DICTIONARY WITH ILLUSTRATED WORDS ON EVERYDAY THEMES
LEARN ARABIC FOR KIDS AND BEGINNER ADULTS

أوّل 500 كلمة باللّغة العربية

Atlas Publishing

FROM THE SAME AUTHOR

ISBN : 979-8-8835-3911-3
Images: freepik.com

CONTACT US

Your suggestions and comments are welcome

https://bio.link/AtlasPeak

If you like our work, please leave us a review on Amazon. Your feedback will be appreciated.

amazon

FOREWORD

This picture book was designed to help children, teens and beginner adults easily learn their first words in the Arabic language.

This glossary contains 570 illustrated words classified into 23 everyday themes: animals, transportation, vehicles, colors, fruits, vegetables, clothes, house, school, numbers, kitchen, bathroom, nature, games, professions, time, geometric shapes...

All words are written in three ways: Arabic letters, pronunciations in Latin letters and English, which makes this picture dictionary book a true bilingual edition. This book can also be used to learn English as a second language.

This English-Arabic visual dictionary is not just a learning tool but also an excellent gift idea for anyone embarking on their language journey. Whether you’re learning Arabic or teaching it to children and beginners, this book is designed to make learning enjoyable and effective.

TABLE OF CONTENTS

ALPHABET الأبجديّة

ج J j Jamal	ث Ṯ ṯ Ṯaɛlab	ت ة T t Tuffaaḥa	ب B b Dubb	أ A a Alf
ر R r Nasr	ذ Ḏ ḏ Ḏahab	د D d Aswad	خ X x [kh] Xamsa	ح Ḥ ḥ Ḥiṣaan
ض Ḍ ḍ Axḍar	ص Ṣ ṣ Aṣfar	ش Š š [sh] Šams	س S s Sitta	ز Z z Manzil
ف F f Fa'r	غ Ɣ ɣ [gh] Ɣazaala	ع Ɛ ɛ Ɛasal	ظ Ḏ ḏ Miḏalla	ط Ṭ ṭ Ṭaa'ira
ن N n Asnaan	م M m Buuma	ل L l Qalam	ك ک K k Kitaab	ق Q q Qird
ا ـَ A a Maa'	ء ʾ Ka's	ي Y y Yadd	و W w Warda	ه ه H h Nahr
	وُ U u [ou] Suuq		ي ـِ I i Diik	

PEOPLE, FAMILY

النّاس والعائلة

رجُل

rajul

Man

امرأة

imra'a

Woman

ولد

walad

Boy

بنت

bint

Girl

أطفال

aṭfaal

Children

رضيع

raḍiiɛ

Baby / infant

النّاس
annaas
People

عائلة
ɛaa'ila
Family

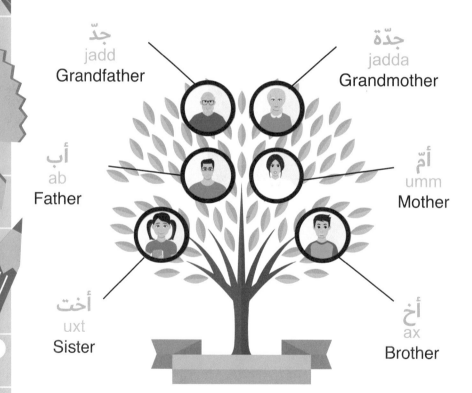

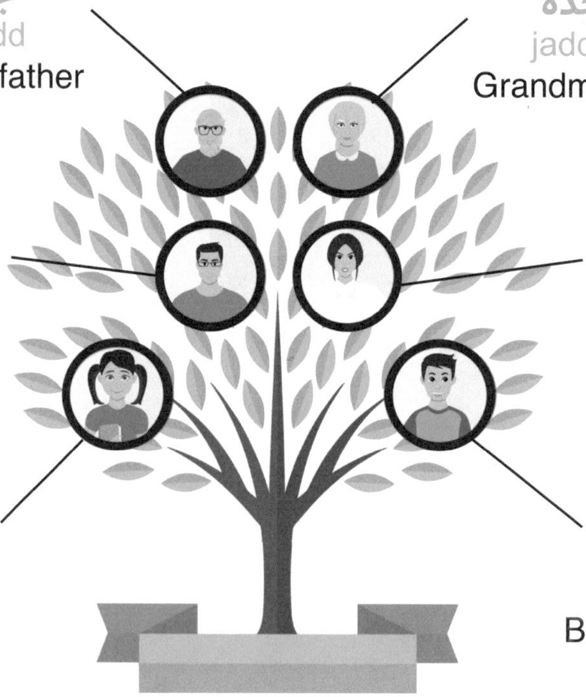

THE BODY
الجسم

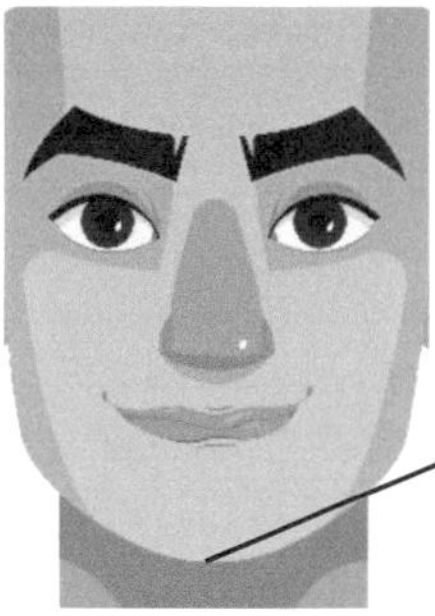

ذقن
daqn
Chin

وجه
wajh
Face

شعر
šaεr
Hair

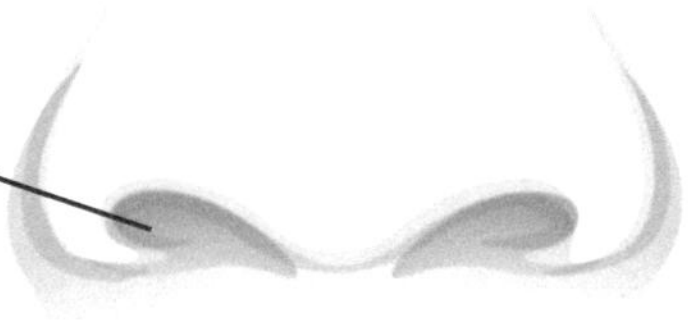

فتحة الأنف
fatḥatu al anf
Nostril

أنف
anf
Nose

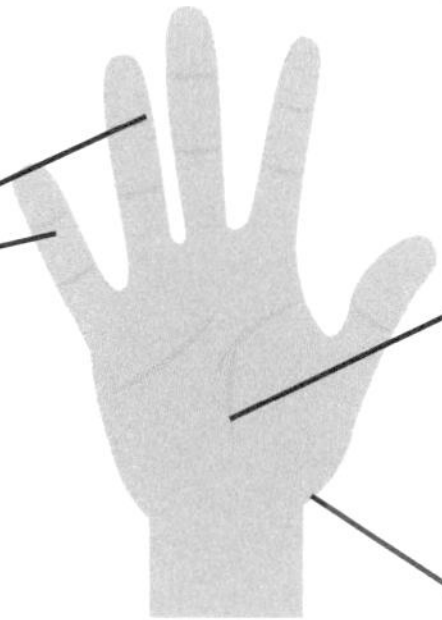

الأصابع
al aṣaabiε
Fingers

كفّ اليد
kaffu al yadd
Palm of the hand

معصم
miεṣam
Wrist

يد
yad
Hand

فم
fam
Mouth

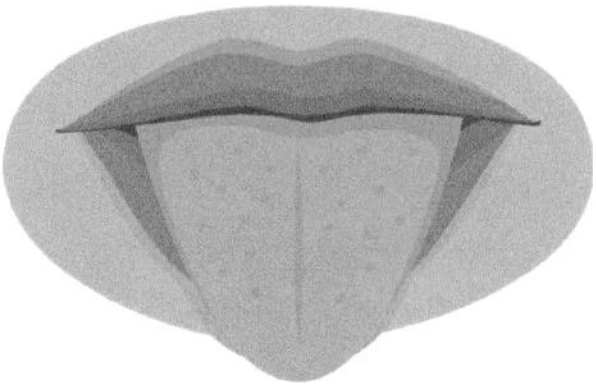

لسان
lisaan
Tongue

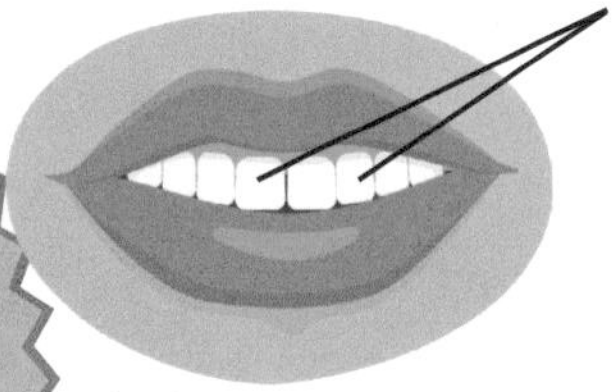

أسنان
asnaan
Teeth

شفاه
šifaah
Lips

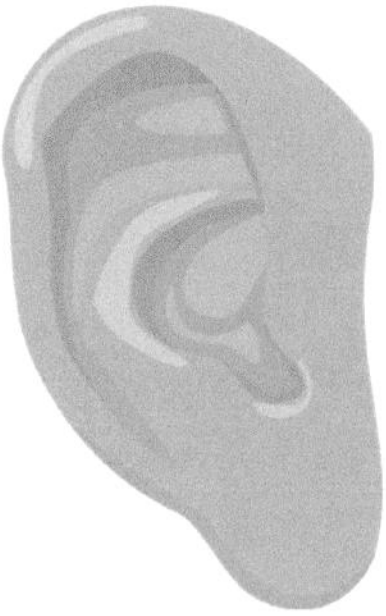

أذن
uḏun
Ear

حواجب
ḥawaajib
Eyebrows

جفن
jafan
Eyelid

رموش العين
rumuuš al
εayn
Eyelashes

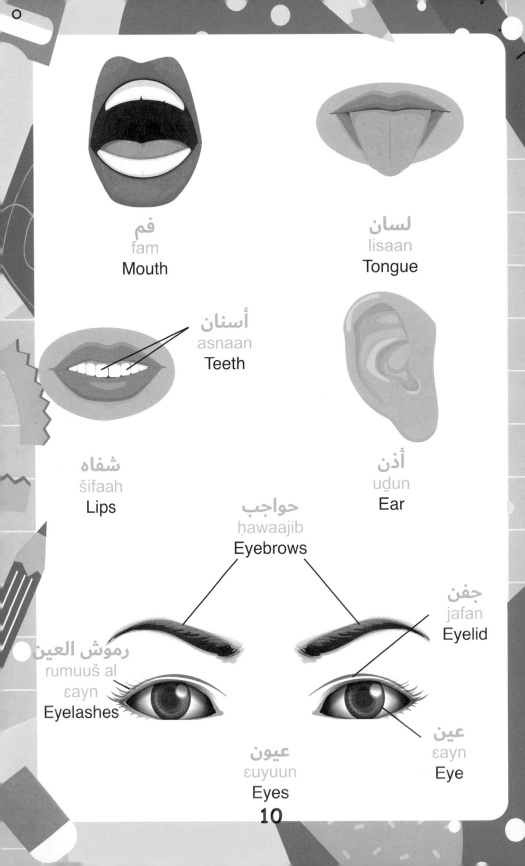

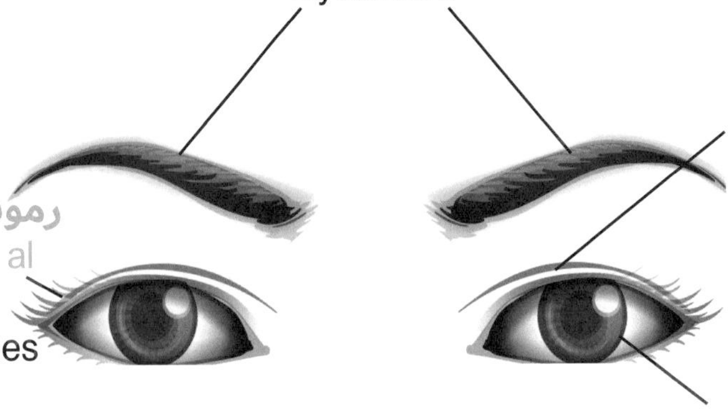

عيون
εuyuun
Eyes

عين
εayn
Eye

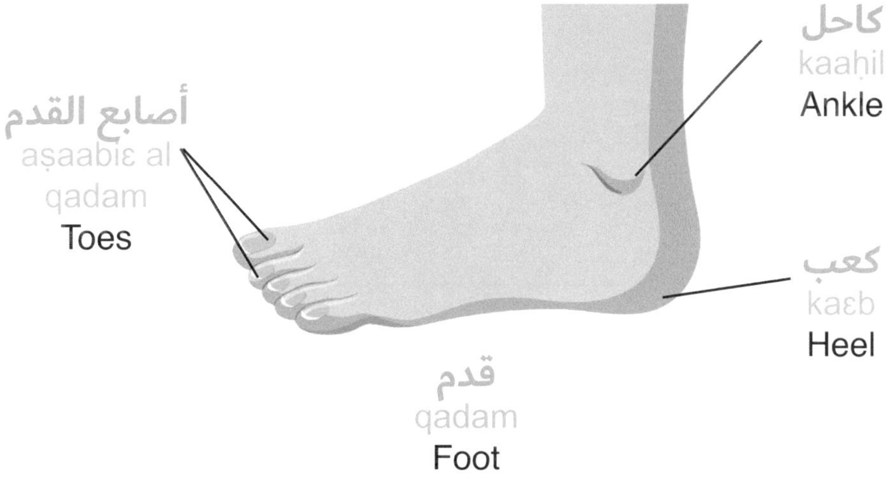
كاحل
kaahil
Ankle
أصابع القدم
aṣaabiɛ al qadam
Toes
كعب
kaɛb
Heel
قدم
qadam
Foot

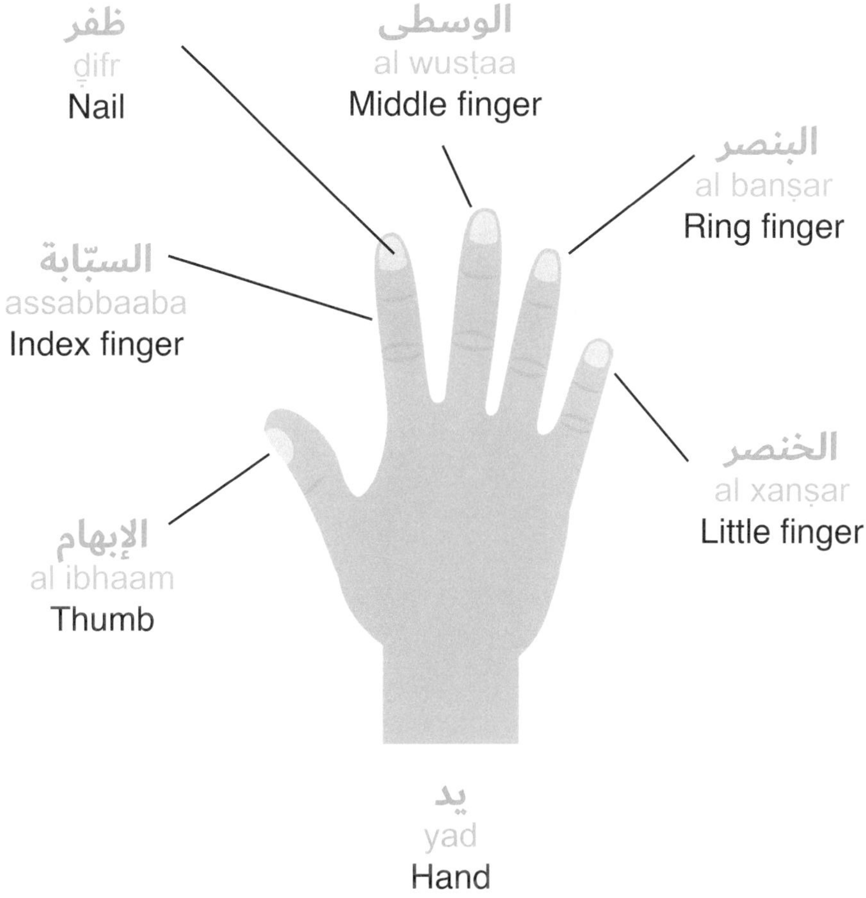
ظفر
ḍifr
Nail
الوسطى
al wusṭaa
Middle finger
البنصر
al banṣar
Ring finger
السبّابة
assabbaaba
Index finger
الخنصر
al xanṣar
Little finger
الإبهام
al ibhaam
Thumb
يد
yad
Hand

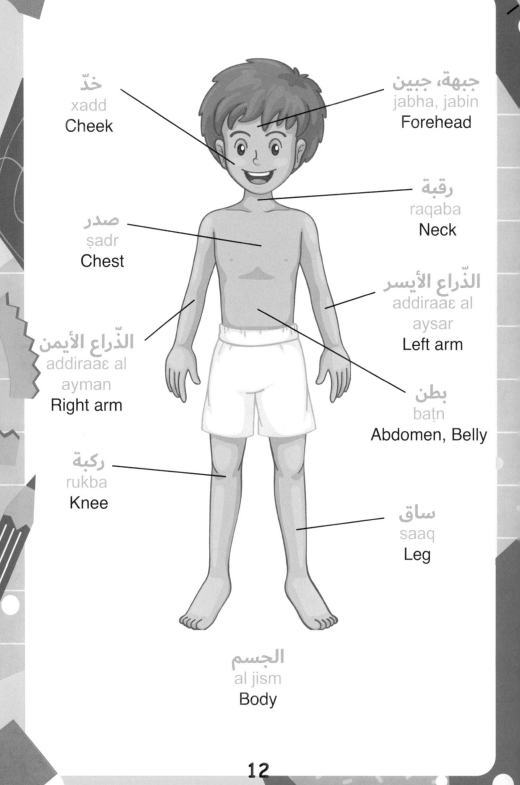

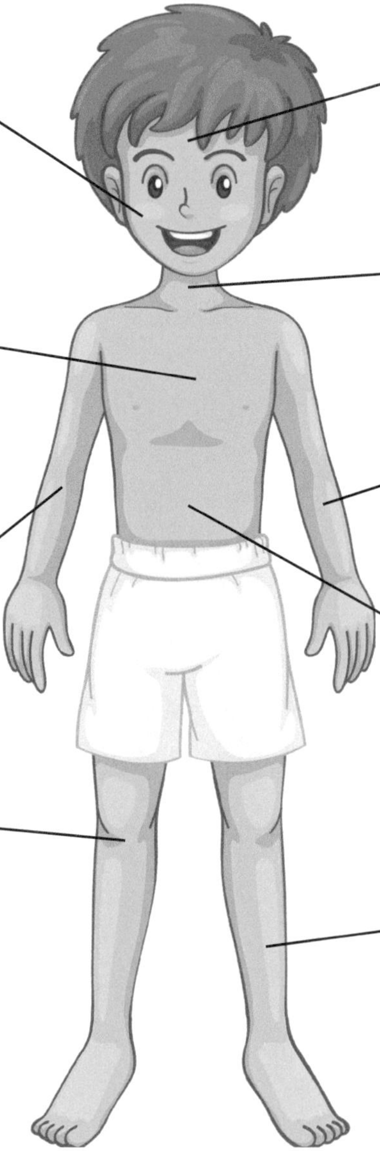
خدّ
xadd
Cheek
جبهة، جبين
jabha, jabin
Forehead
رقبة
raqaba
Neck
صدر
ṣadr
Chest
الذّراع الأيسر
addiraaɛ al aysar
Left arm
الذّراع الأيمن
addiraaɛ al ayman
Right arm
بطن
baṭn
Abdomen, Belly
ركبة
rukba
Knee
ساق
saaq
Leg

الجسم
al jism
Body

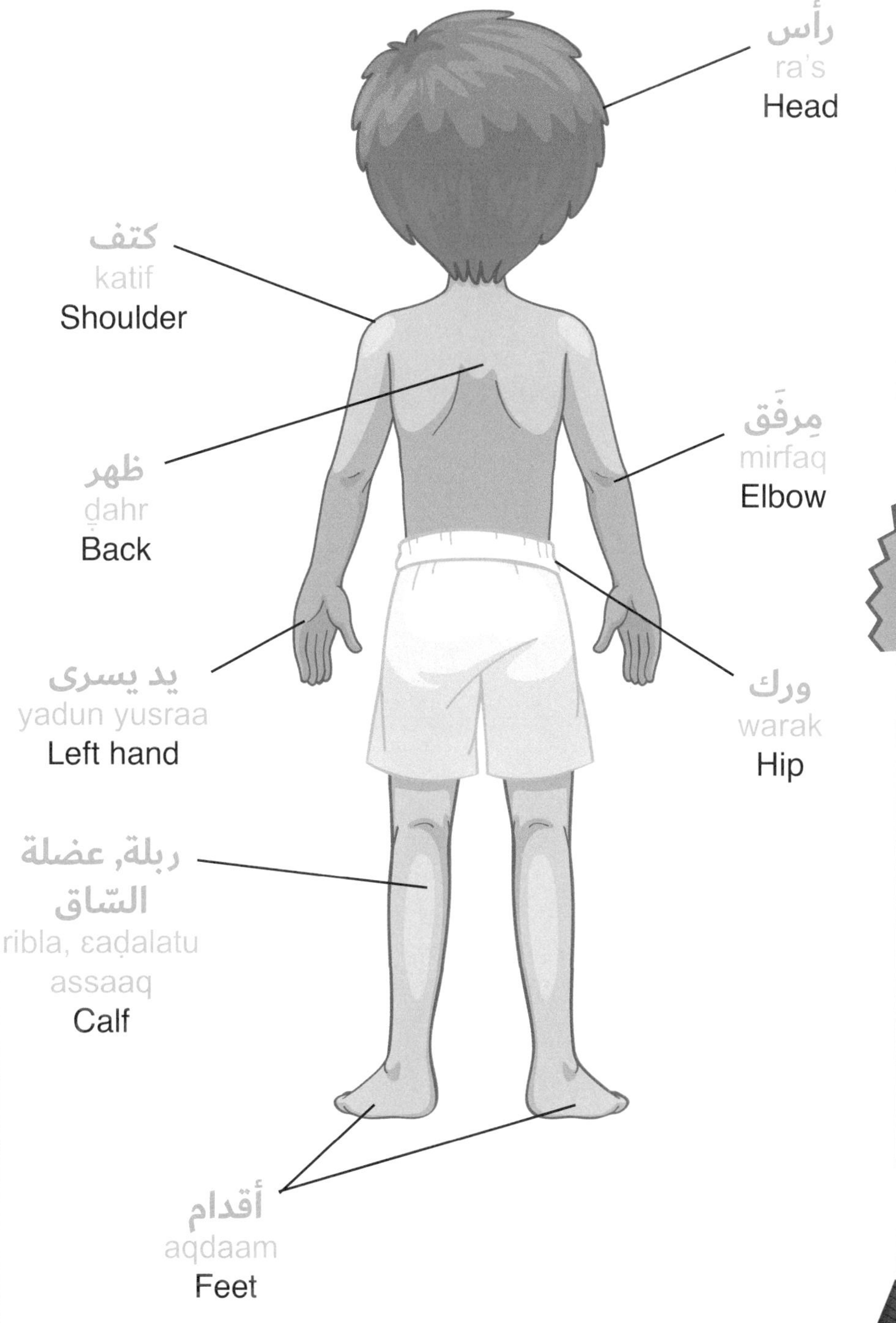
رأس
ra's
Head
كتف
katif
Shoulder
مِرفَق
mirfaq
Elbow
ظهر
ḍahr
Back
يد يسرى
yadun yusraa
Left hand
ورك
warak
Hip
ربلة, عضلة السّاق
ribla, ɛaḍalatu assaaq
Calf
أقدام
aqdaam
Feet

FRUITS AND VEGETABLES
الفواكه و الخضر

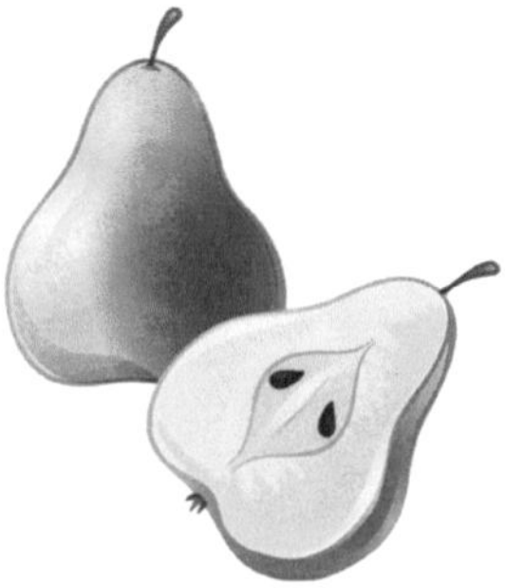

إجّاص
ijjaaṣ
Pear

موزة
mawza
Banana

خوخ
xuux
Peach

بطّيخة
battiixa
Watermelon

عنب
ɛinab
Grape

تين
tiin
Fig

تفّاحة

tuffaaḥa

Apple

برتقالة

burtuqaala

Orange

فراولة

faraawla

Strawberry

أناناس

ananas

Pineapple

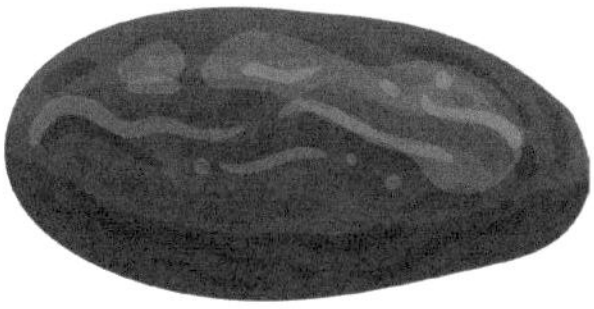

تمرة

tamara

Date

زيتونة

zaytuuna

Olive

لَيْمونة حَامِضة
laymuuna ḥaamiḍa
Lemon, lime

رمّانة
rammaana
Pomegranate

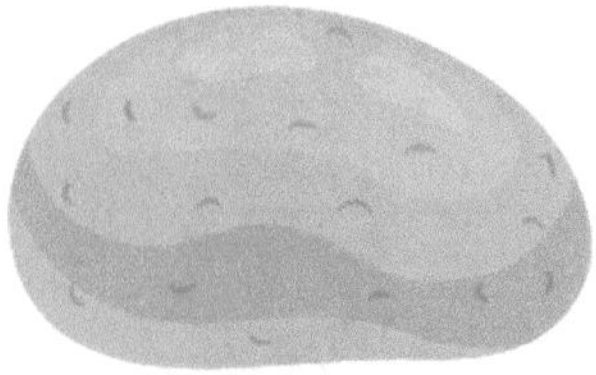

بطاطس
baṭaaṭis
Potato

طماطم
ṭamaaṭim
Tomato

جزرة
jazara
Carrot

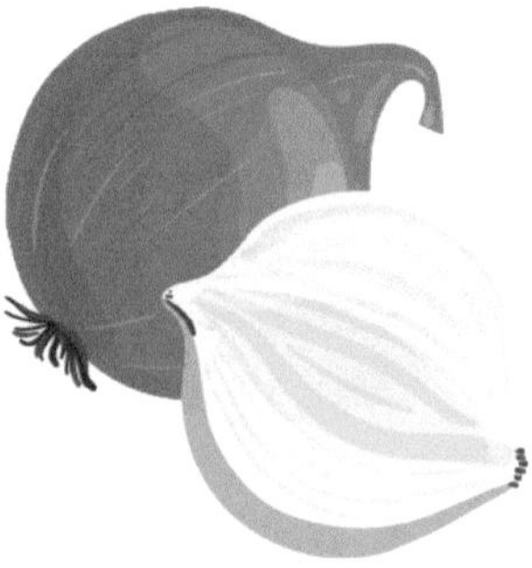

بصلة
baṣala
Onion

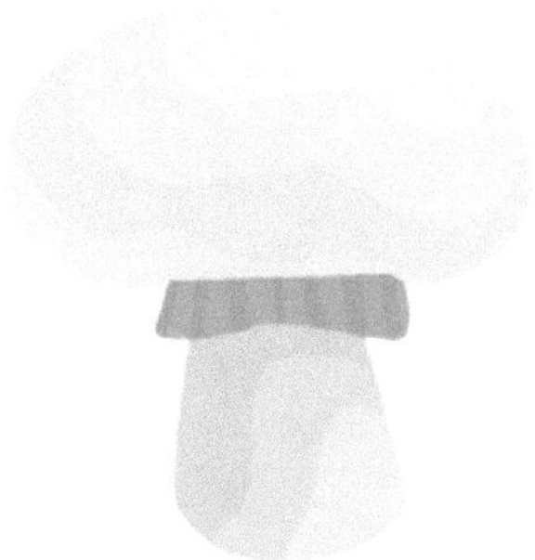

فطر
fiṭr
Mushroom

يقطين
yaqṭiin
Pumpkin

ثوم
ṯuum
Garlic

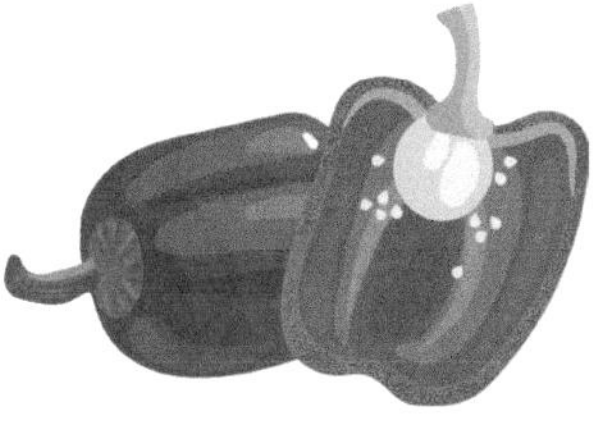

فلفل حلو
filfil ḥilu
Sweet pepper, bell pepper

لوز
luuz
Almonds

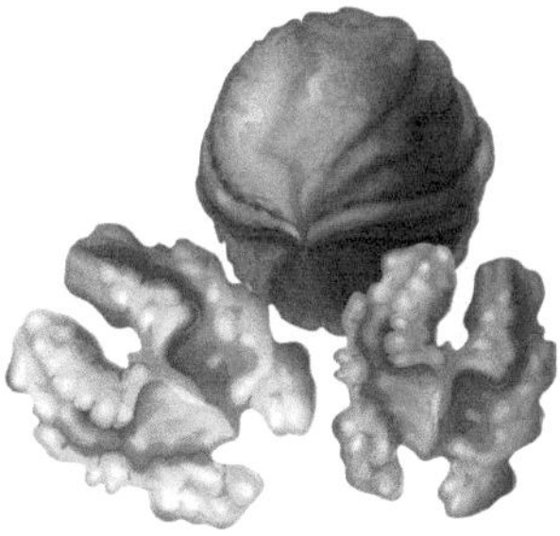

جوز
jawz
Walnut

قرنبيط
qarnabiiṭ
Cauliflower

بازيلاء
baaziila'
Peas

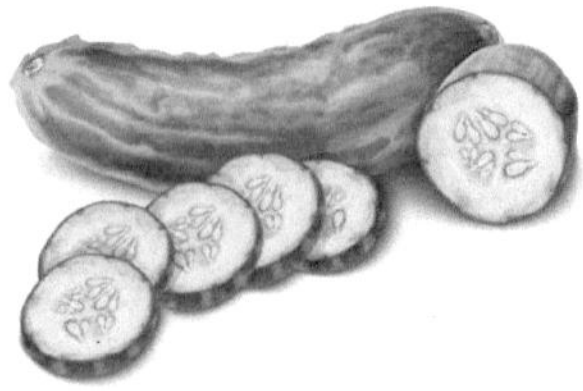

خيار
xiyaar
Cucumber

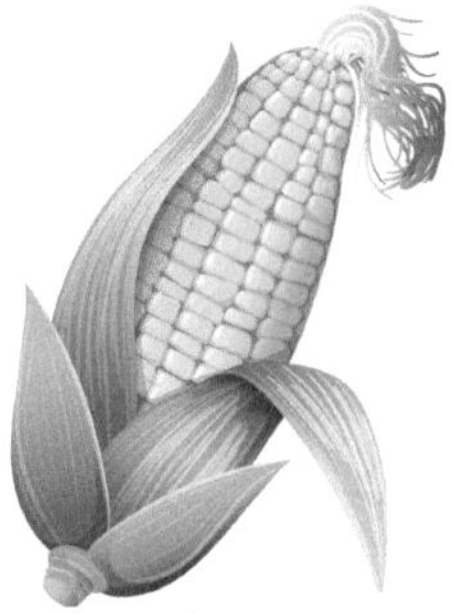

كوز الذّرة
kawz aḏḏura
Corncob

كرنب
kurnub
Cabbage

كوسة
kuusa
Zucchini

FOOD
الأغذية

حليب
ḥaliib
Milk

سلطة
salṭa
Salad

زبادي, يوغرت
zabadii, yuuɣurt
Yogurt

بيضة
bayḍa
Egg

دقيق
daqiiq
Flour

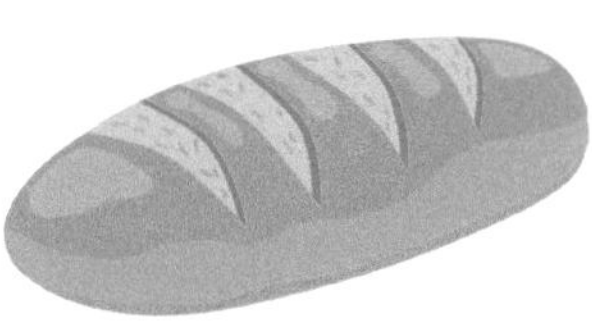

خبز
xubz
Bread

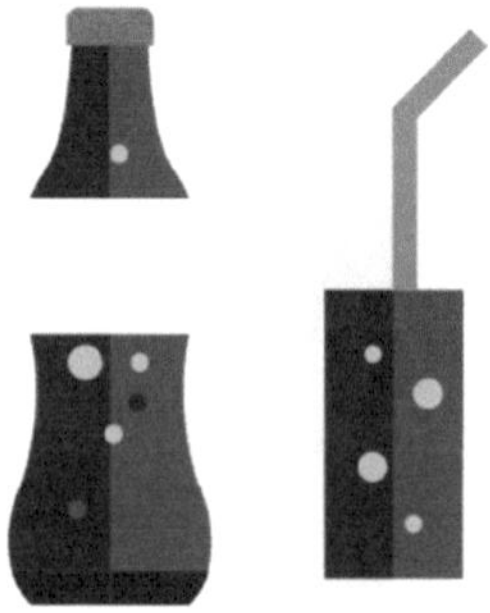

مشروب
mašruub
Beverage, drink

عصير
εaṣiir
Juice

سكّر
sukkar
Sugar

زيت الزّيتون
zayt azzaytuun
Olive oil

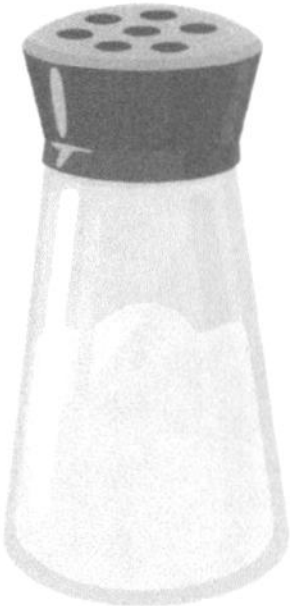

ملح
milḥ
Salt

فلفل أسود
filfil aswad
Pepper

حلويّات
ḥalawiyyaat
Candy

بسكويت
biskawiit
Biscuit

عسل
ɛasal
Honey

مربّى
murabbaa
Jam

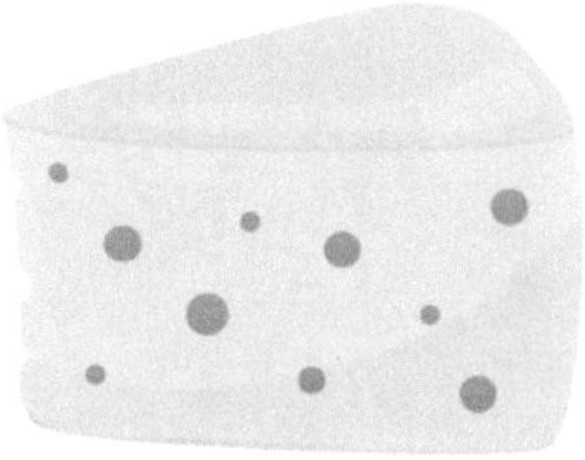

جبنة
jubna
Cheese

زبدة
zubda
Butter

مثلّجات, آيس كريم
muṯallajaat, ays kriim
Ice cream

قشدة
qišda
Cream

لحم
laḥm
Meat

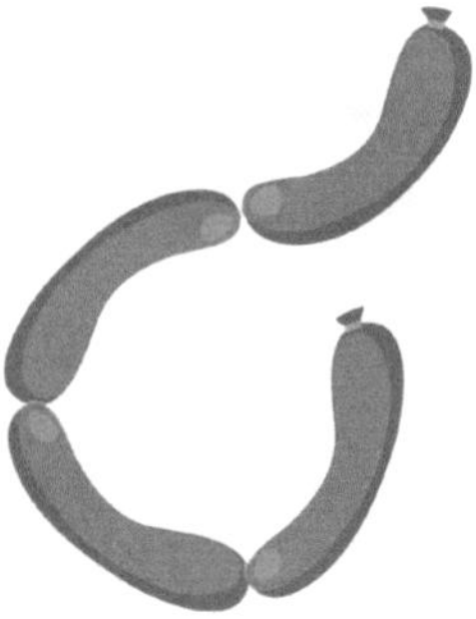

نقانق
naqaaniq
Sausages

أكل
akl
to eat

شرب
šurb
to drink

CLOTHES

الملابس

قبّعة, كاب
qubbaεa, kaab
Cap

قبّعة بيني
qubbaεatu biinii
Beanie

قفّازات
qaffaazat
Gloves

مظلّة
miḍalla
Umbrella

ساعة يد
saaεatu yadd
Watch

نظّارات
naḍḍaaraat
Glasses

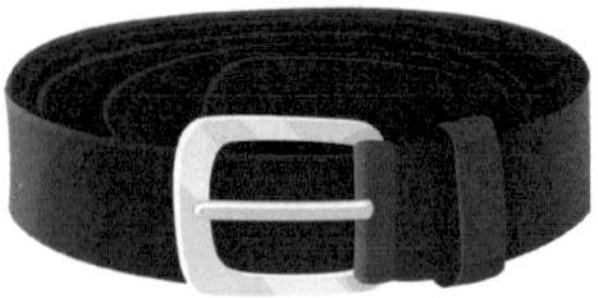

حزام
ḥizaam
Belt

جوارب
jawaarib
Socks

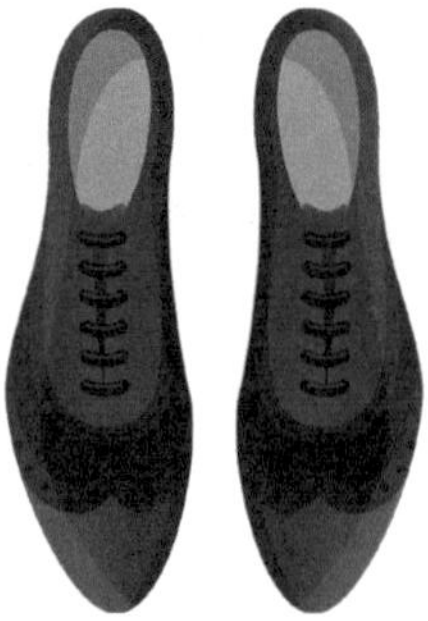

أحذية
aḥḏiya
Shoes

حِذَاءٌ رياضي
ḥiḏa'un riyaaḍi
Sneakers / athletic shoes

حِذَاءٌ مَطَّاطيّ
ḥiḏaa' maṭṭaaṭi
Rain boots / rubber boots

صنادل
ṣanaadil
Sandals

سُترة, بُلُوزَةٌ صُوفِيّة

sutra, buluza ṣufiyya

Sweater

جاكيت

jaakiit

Jacket

تي شيرت

tii šiirt

T-shirt

قميص

qamiiṣ

Shirt

سروال, بنطلون

sirwaal, banṭaluun

Pants

سروال قصير

sirwaal qaṣir

Shorts

تنّورة
tannuura
Skirt

معطف واق من المطر
miɛṭafun waaqin mina al maṭar
Raincoat

مِئْزَر
mi’zar
Apron

سروال داخلي
sirwaal daaxili
Briefs / panties

لباس السِّباحة
libaas assibaaḥa
Swimsuit

لباس النّوم ,بيجامة
libaas annawm, biijaama
Pyjamas / pajamas

TRANSPORTATION

وسائل النّقل

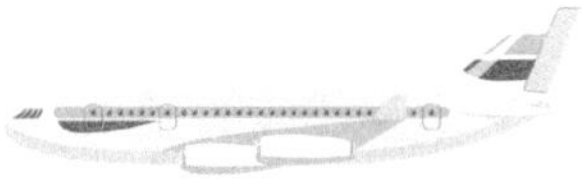

طائرة

ṭaa'ira

Plane / aircraft

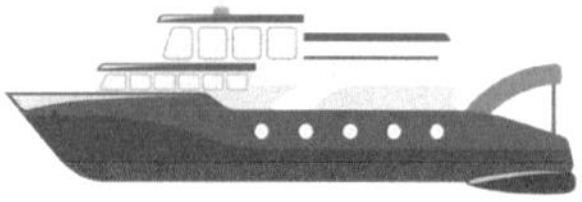

قارب, سفينة

qaarib, safiina

Boat / ship

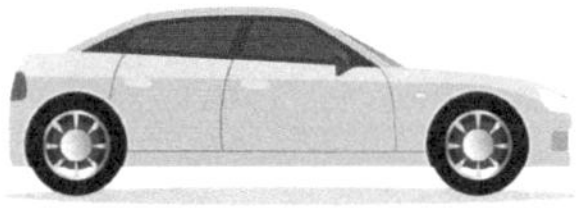

سيّارة

sayyaara

Car

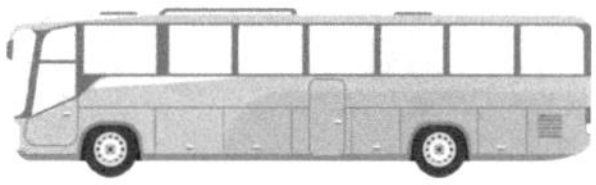

حافلة

ḥaafila

Bus

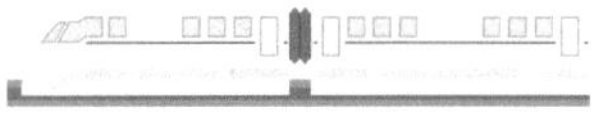

قطار

qiṭaar

Train

شاحنة

šaaḥina

Truck

درّاجة ناريّة صغيرة
darraaja naariyya ṣaɣiira
Moped / motorcycle

درّاجة ناريّة
darraaja naariyya
Motorbike / bike

درّاجة هوائيّة
darraaja hawaa'iyya
Bicycle

جرّار
jarraar
Tractor

زورق
zawraq
Rowboat

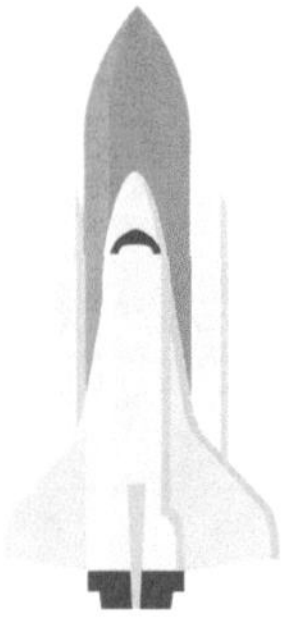

صاروخ
ṣaaruux
Rocket

AT HOME

في المنزل

منزل, دار
manzil, daar
House

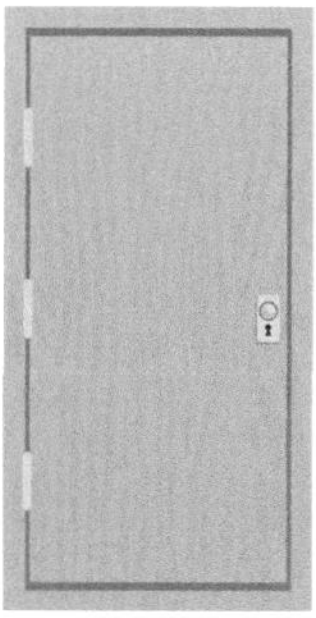

باب
baab
Door

ستارة
sitaara
Curtain

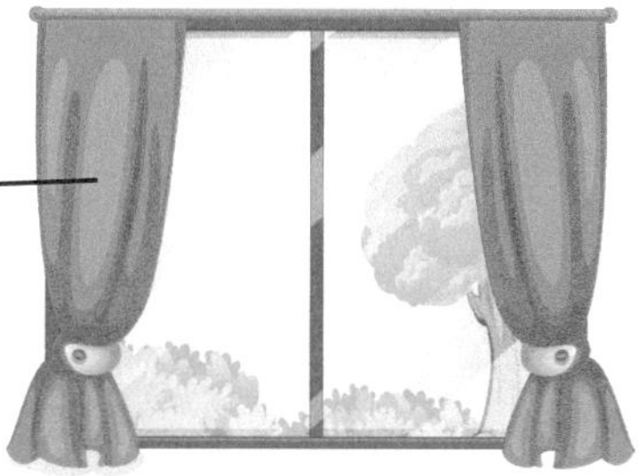

نافذة
naafiḏa
Window

بطّانية, غطاء
baṭṭaaniyya, ɣiṭaa'
Blanket

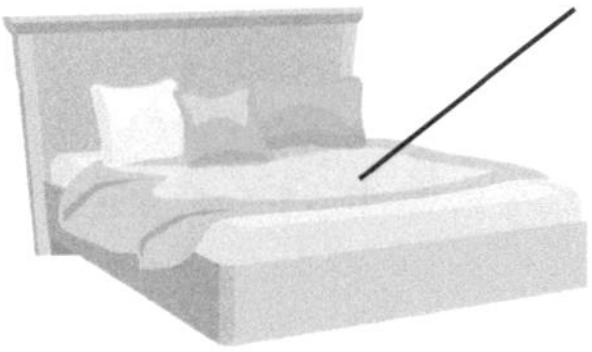

سرير
sariir
Bed

كرسي
kursii
Chair

أريكة
ariika
Couch, armchair

وسادة
wisaada
Pillow / cushion

طاولة
ṭaawila
Table

خزانة
xizaana
Wardrobe

تلفزيون
tilifizyuun
TV

جهاز التّحكم عن بعد
jihaaz attaḥakkum ɛan buɛd
Remote control

مفتاح
miftaaḥ
Key

مصباح
miṣbaaḥ
Light bulb

مشبك الملابس
mišbak al malaabis
Clothespin [US]
Clothes peg [GB]

منشار
minšaar
Saw

مكنسة
miknasa
Broom

سُلّم
sullam
Ladder

مطرقة ثقيلة
miṭraqa ṯaqiila
Sledgehammer

مطرقة
miṭraqa
Hammer

حبل
ḥabl
Rope

مفكّ البراغي
mifakku al baraaɣii
Screwdriver

مِجْرَفَة
mijrafa
Shovel

دواء
dawaa'
Medicine

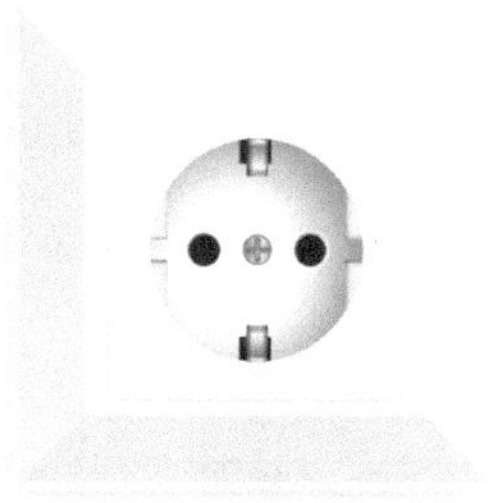

مقبس كهربائي
miqbas kahrabaa'i
Outlet US
Socket GB

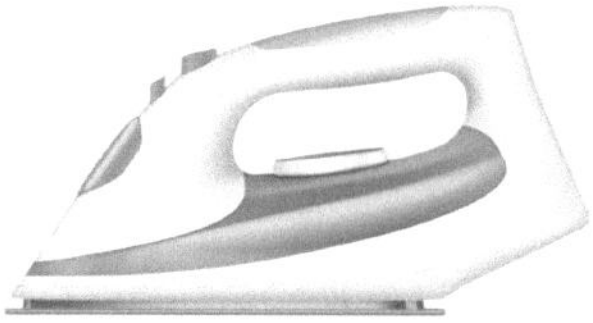

مِكْوَاة
mikwaat
Iron

دلو
dalw
Bucket

صنبور
ṣunbuur
Faucet

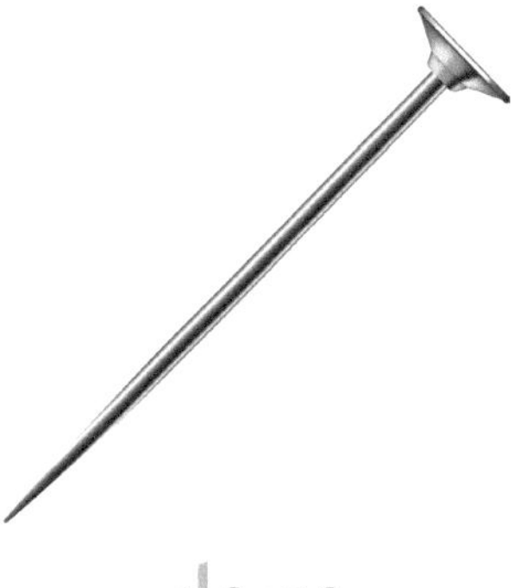

مسمار
mismaar
Nail

سجّادة، زربيّة
sajjaada, zarbiyya
Carpet

KITCHEN مطبخ

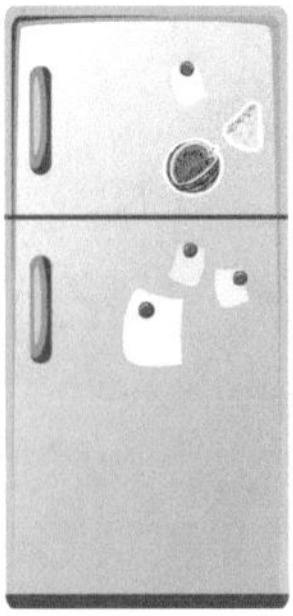

ثلّاجة
ṯallaaja
Fridge

مِقلاة
miqlaat
Pan

ملعقة
milɛaqa
Spoon

شوكة
šawka
Fork

سكّين
sikkiin
Knife

كأس
ka’s
Glass

سُلْطَانِيَّة

ṣulṭaaniyya

Bowl

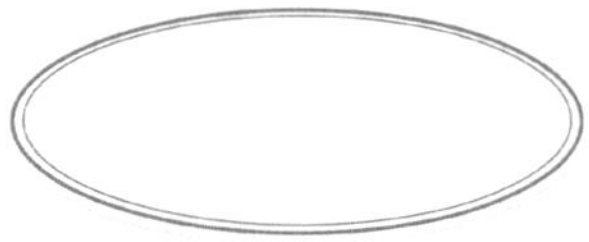

طبق

ṭabaq

Plate

قارورة, قِنِّينَة

qaaruura, qinniina

Bottle

منشفة

minšafa

Dish towel, dish cloth

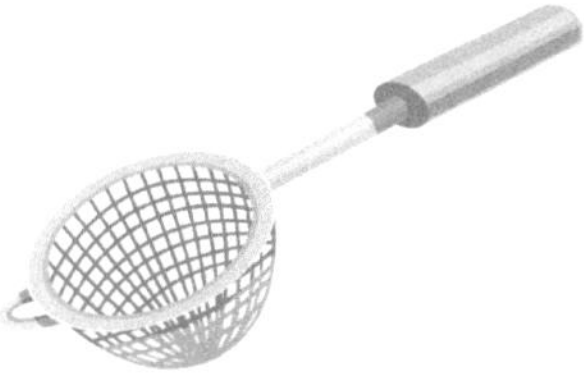

مصفاة

miṣfaat

Strainer, filter

وَلّاعة

wallaaεa

Lighter

صينيّة

ṣiiniyya

Tray

إبريق حراري, تِرموس

ibriqun ḥaraari, tirmuus

Thermos

غلّاية

ɣallaaya

Kettle

موقد غاز

mawqidu ɣaaz

Gas stove

فرن

furn

Oven

مغسلة المطبخ

miɣsalatu al maṭbax

Kitchen sink

BATHROOM

حمّام

فوطة

fuuṭa

Towel

مرآة

mir'aat

Mirror

مشط

mišṭ

Comb

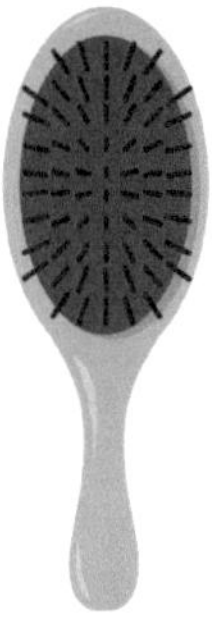

فرشاة للشّعر ،مشط

furšaat liššaɛr, mišṭ

Hair brush

معجون الأسنان

maɛjuun al asnaan

Toothpaste

فرشاة الأسنان

furšaat al asnaan

Toothbrush

شامبو
šambuu
Shampoo

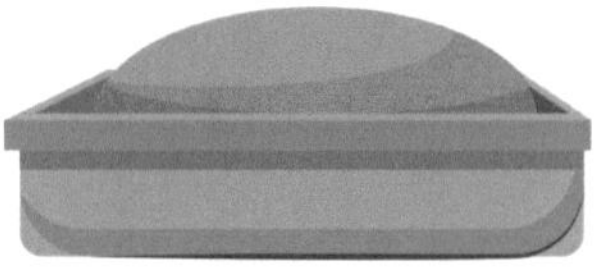

صابون
ṣaabuun
Soap

دش, مِرَشَّةُ الحَمّامِ
duš, miraššatu al ḥammaam
Shower

مجفّف الشّعر
mujaffifu aššaεr
Hair dryer

حوض الغسل, مغسلة
ḥawḍu al ɣasl, miɣsala
Washbasin / Sink

مرحاض
mirḥaaḍ
Toilet, restroom

SCHOOL

في المدرسة

مدرسة
madrasa
School

قسم
qism
Classroom

مدرِّس
mudarris
Teacher

مدرِّسة
mudarrisa
Teacher (f)

تلميذة
tilmiiḏa
Student / pupil (f)

تلميذ
tilmiiḏ
Student / pupil

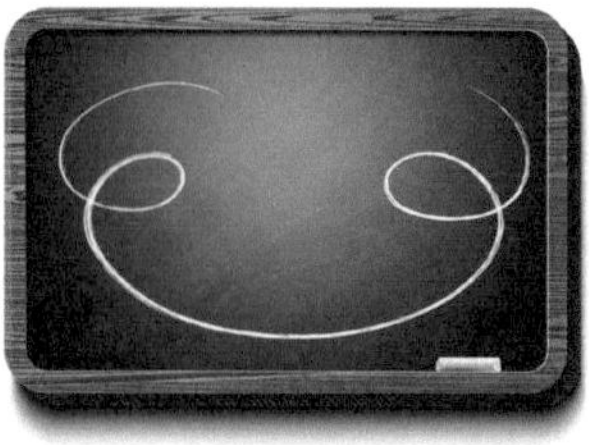

لوحة
lawḥa
Slate / Chalkboard

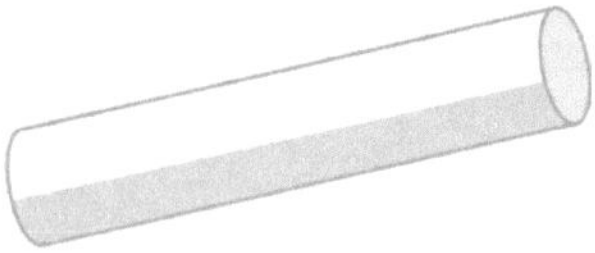

طباشير
ṭabaašiir
Chalk

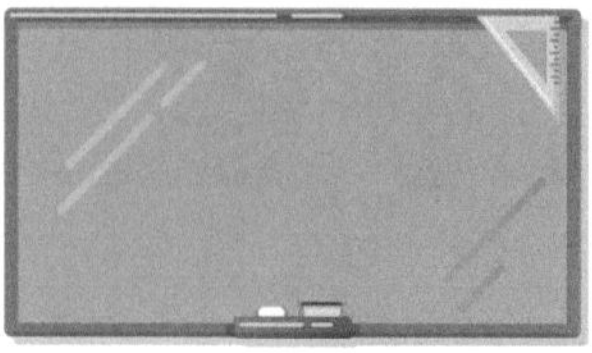

سبّورة
sabbuura
Board, blackboard

طاولة
ṭaawila
Table

قلم
qalam
Pencil

أقلام التّلوين
aqlaamu attalwiin
Colouring pencils

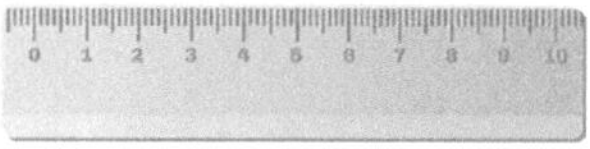

مسطرة
misṭara
Ruler

فرشاة
furšaat
Brush

ممحاة
mimḥaat
Eraser

مقلمة
miqlama
Pencil case

دفتر
diftar
Notebook

كتاب
kitaab
Book

قلم حبر
qalamu ḥibr
Pen

حقيبة مدرسيّة
ḥaqiiba madrasiyya
School bag, backpack

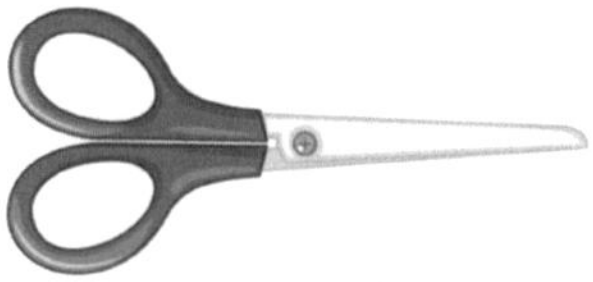

مقصّ
miqaṣṣ
Scissors

مِبْراةُ الأَقْلامِ
mibraatu al aqlaam
Pencil sharpener

حاسوب
ḥaasuub
Computer

حاسوب محمول
ḥaasuub maḥmuul
Laptop

قاموس، معجم
qaamuus, muεjam
Dictionary

آلة حاسبة
aalatun ḥaasiba
Calculator

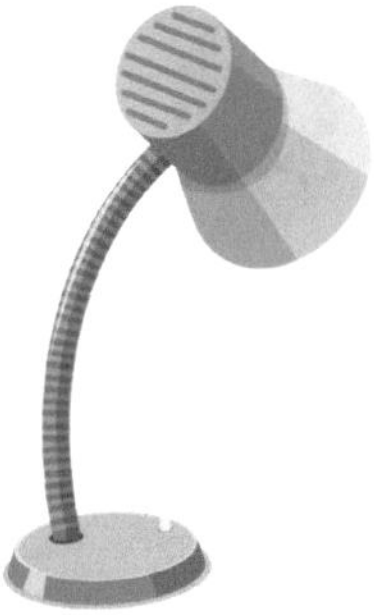

مصباح المكتب
miṣbaaḥu al maktab
Lamp

غراء
ɣiraa’
Glue

مجهر
mijhar
Microscope

تلسكوب
tiliskuub
Telescope

ANIMALS

الحيوانات

بَبّغاء
babbaɣaa’
Parrot

سلحفاة
sulaḥfaat
Tortoise

كلب
kalb
Dog

قطّة
qiṭṭa
Cat

أرنب
arnab
Rabbit

فأر
fa’r
Mouse

دجاجة
dajaaja
Chicken

ديك
diik
Rooster

كتكوت
katkuut
Chick

حمامة
ḥamaama
Pigeon

بطّة
baṭṭa
Duck

حصان
ḥiṣaan
Horse

بقرة
baqara
Cow

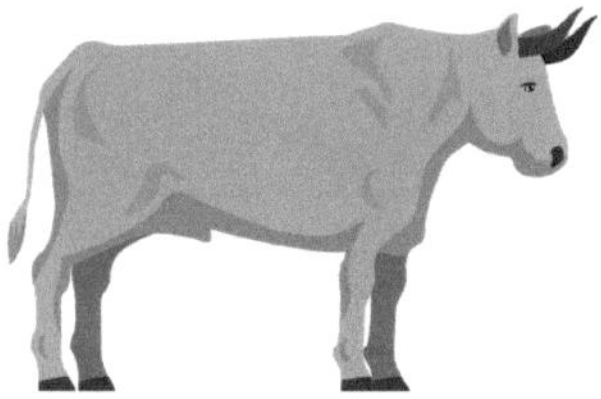

ثور
t̲awr
Bull

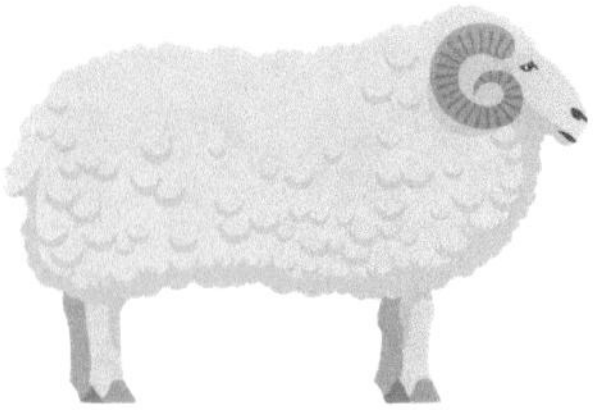

خروف
xaruuf
Sheep

حمار
ḥimaar
Donkey

معزة
maεza
Goat

خنزير
xinziir
Pig

تمساح
timsaaḥ
Crocodile

ثعبان
ṯuεbaan
Snake

ضفدع
ḍifdaε
Frog

سحليّة , أبو بريص
saḥliyya, abu briiṣ
Lizard / gecko

حَلزون
ḥalazuun
Snail

حِرباء
ḥirbaa’
Chameleon

طائر
ṭaa'ir
Bird

نعّامة
naɛɛaama
Ostrich

بُومَة
buuma
Owl

نسر
nasr
Eagle

لقلاق
laqlaaq
Stork

صقر
ṣaqr
Falcon

نمر
namir
Tiger

ثعلب
ṯaεlab
Fox

ابن آوى
ibn aawa
Jackal

ذئب
ḏi'b
Wolf

فهد
fahd
Leopard

نمر أسود
namir aswad
Panther

أسد
asad
Lion

قنفذ
qunfuḏ
Hedgehog

دُبّ
dubb
Bear

ضبع
ḍabɛ
Hyena

جمل
jamal
Dromedary / camel

قرد
qird
Monkey

غزالة

ɣazaala

Gazelle

أيّل

ayyil

Deer

فيل

fiil

Elephant

زرافة

zaraafa

Giraffe

أرنب برّي

arnab barri

Hare

خنزير برّي

xinzir barri

Wild boar

سمكة

samaka

Fish

سمك القرش

samak al qirš

Shark

حوت

ḥuut

Whale

أخطبوط

uxṭubuuṭ

Octopus

دلفين

dulfiin

Dolphin

أَنْقَلَيْس

anqalays

Eel

سرطان البحر
saraṭaan al baḥr
Crab

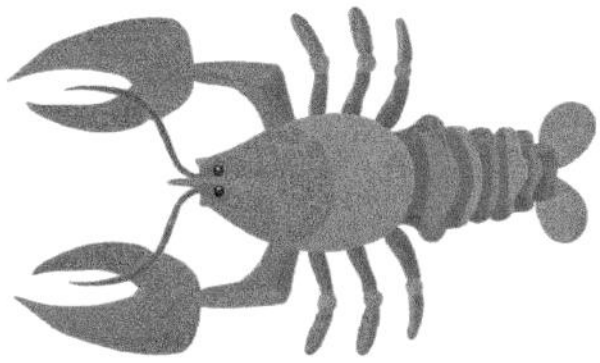

كَرْكَنْد, جراد البحر
karkand, jaraad al baḥr
Lobster

جمبري
jambarii
Shrimp

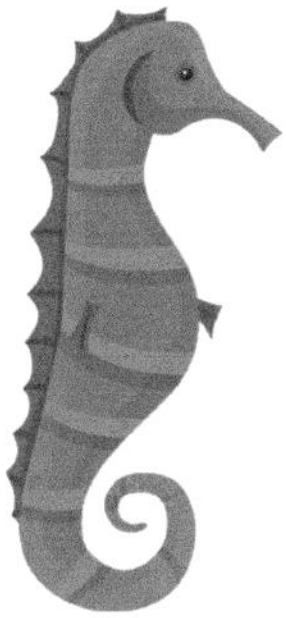

فرس البحر
farasu al baḥr
Seahorse

فُقْمَة
fuqma
Seal

فرس النهر
farasu annahr
Hippopotamus

INSECTS

الحشرات

نحلة
naḥla
Bee

دعسوقة
daɛsuuqa
Ladybug

فراشة
faraaša
Butterfly

نملة
namla
Ant

بعوضة
baɛuuḍa
Mosquito

ذُبَابَة
ḏubaaba
Fly

عنكبوت
ɛankabuut
Spider

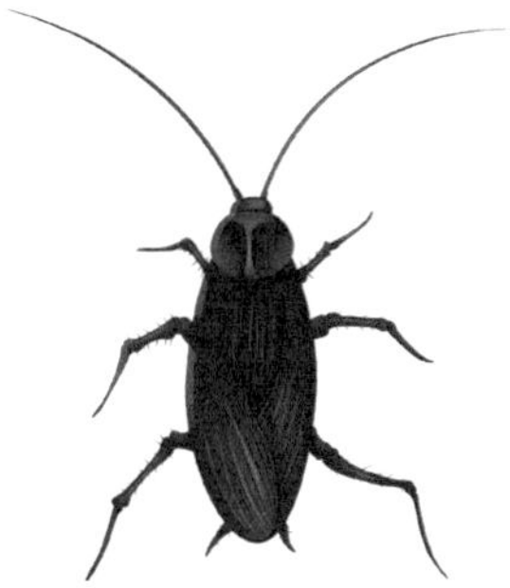

صرصور
ṣarṣuur
Cockroach

دُودَة
duuda
Worm

عقرب
ɛaqrab
Scorpion

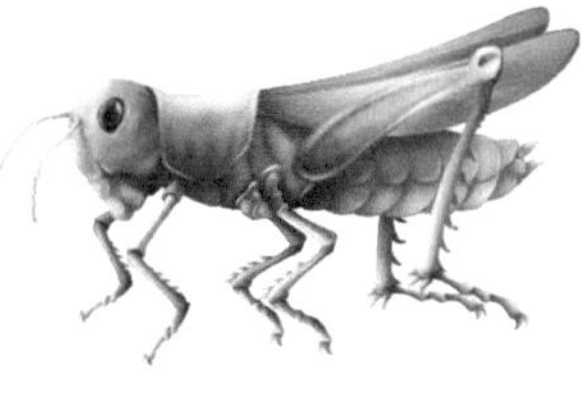

جرادة
jaraada
Grasshopper

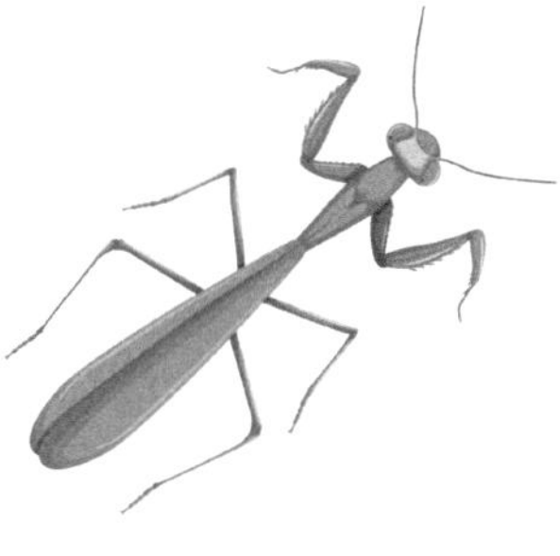

سرعوف
surɛuuf
Praying mantis

NEIGHBORHOOD الحيّ

مبنى
mabnaa
Building

منزل
manzil
House

سوق
suuq
Market

محل بقّالة
maḥal baqqaala
Convenience store

مطعم
maṭɛam
Restaurant

مخبزة
maxbaza
Bakery

مدرسة
madrasa
School

ثانويّة إعداديّة
taanawiyya iɛdaadiyya
Middle school

ثانويّة
taanawiyya
High school

جامعة
jaamiɛa
University

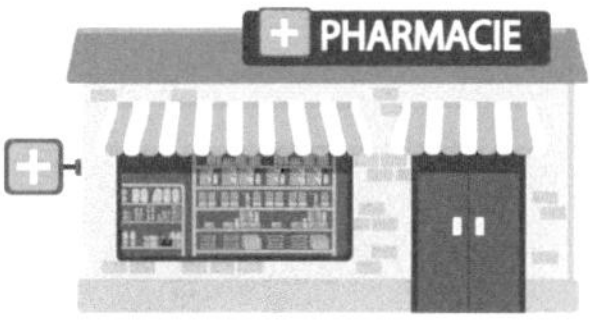

صيدليّة
ṣaydaliyya
Pharmacy / drugstore

مكتبة
maktaba
Library

مسجد
masjid
Mosque

كنيسة
kaniisa
Church

مستشفى
mustašfaa
Hospital

مفترق طرق
muftaraqu aṭṭuruq
Crossroads / intersection

طريق
ṭariiq
Road

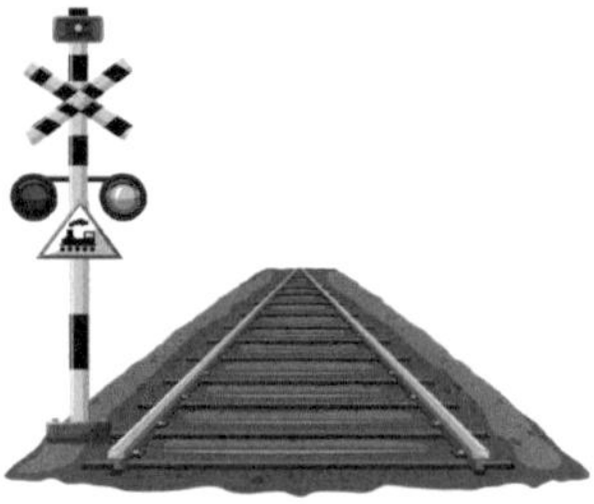

سكة حديديّة
sikka ḥadiidiyya
Railway

اضواء المرور
aḍwaa’ al muruur
Traffic lights

معبر المشاة
maεbaru al mušaat
Pedestrian crossing, zebra crossing

المال، العملة
al maal, al εumla
Money / currency

رصيف
raṣiif
Sidewalk

اشارات حركة المرور
išaaraat ḥarakat al muruur
Traffic signs

مصعد
miṣεad
Elevator

NATURE

الطّبيعة

شجرة
šajara
Tree

غابة
ɣaaba
Forest

نبتة
nabta
Plant

وردة
warda
Flower

حديقة
ḥadiiqa
Garden

قوس قزح
qawsu quzaḥ
Rainbow

ربيع
rabiiɛ
Spring

صيف
ṣayf
Summer

الفصول
al fuṣuul
Seasons

شتاء
šitaa'
Winter

خريف
xariif
Autumn

نهر
nahr
River

جبل
jabal
Mountain

العالم، الأرض
al ɛaalam, al arḍ
World / Earth

شمس
šams
Sun

بدر كامل
badrun kaamil
Full moon

قمر
qamar
Moon

نجوم
nujuum
Stars

مطر
maṭar
Rain

برق
barq
Lightning

ثلج
ṯalj
Snow

سحاب
saḥaab
Cloud

صخرة
ṣaxra
Rock

بحر
baḥr
Sea

سماء
samaa'
Sky

شاطئ
šaaṭi'
Beach

ماء
maa’
Water

نار
naar
Fire

أرض, تربة
arḍ, turba
Soil

خشب
xašab
Wood

جليد
jaliid
Ice

هواء
hawaa’
Air

عين, منبع
ɛayn, manbaɛ
Spring, water source

شلّال
šallaal
Waterfall

جزيرة
jaziira
Island

ضباب
ḍabaab
Fog

رياح
riyaaḥ
Wind

ضوء
ḍaw'
Light

نهار
nahaar
Day

ليل
layl
Night

شمال
šamaal
North

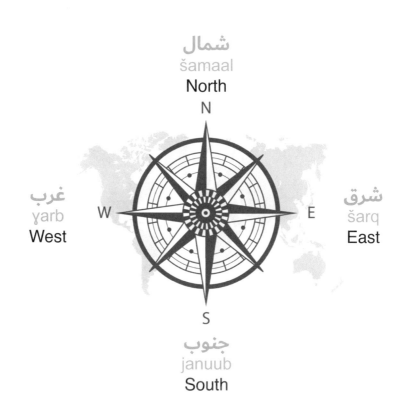

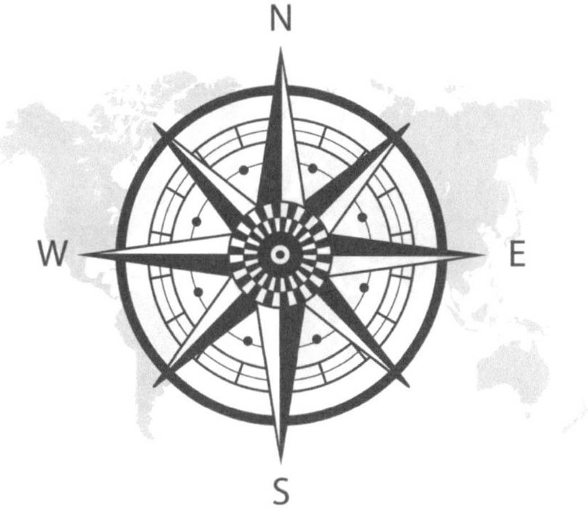

غرب
ɣarb
West

شرق
šarq
East

جنوب
januub
South

METALS

المعادن

ذهب
ḏahab
Gold

حديد
ḥadiid
Iron

فضّة
fiḍḍa
Silver

نحاس
nuḥaas
Copper

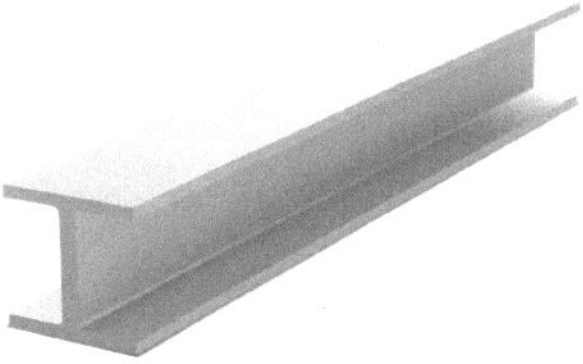

فُولاَذ
fuulaaḏ
Steel

برونز
bruunz
Bronze

PROFESSIONS

المهن

مهندس معماري
muhandis miεmaarii
Architect

مهندس
muhandis
Engineer

طبيبة
ṭabiiba
Doctor

طبيب أسنان
ṭabiib al asnaan
Dentist

طبيب بيطري
ṭabiib bayṭarii
Veterinarian

أستاذة
ustaaḏa
Teacher (f)

حدّاد

ḥaddaad

Black-smith

فنّان

fannaan

Artist

خبّاز

xabbaaz

Baker

جزّار

jazzaar

Butcher

أمينة الصّندوق, صرّافة

amiinatu assunduuq, ṣarraafa

Cashier

ساعي البريد

saaεii al bariid

Postman

سبّاك
sabbaak
Plumber

سائق
saa'iq
Driver

حلّاق
ḥallaaq
Barber, hairdresser

ممرّضة
mumarriḍa
Nurse

رئيسة الطّهاة
ra'iisatu aṭṭuhaat
Head chef

فلّاح
fallaaḥ
Farmer

رجل الإطفاء
rajul al iṭfaa’
Firefighter

ضابط شرطة
ḍaabiṭ šurṭa
Police officer, policeman

جندي
jundii
Soldier

صحافيّة
ṣaḥaafiyya
Journalist

بنّاء
bannaa’
Mason, builder

ميكانيكي
miikaaniikii
Mechanic

طيّار
ṭayyaar
Pilot

مصوّر فوتوغرافي
muṣawwir futuɣraafii
Photographer

نادلة
naadila
Waitress

حرفي
ḥirafii
Artisan, craftsman

صيّاد السمك
ṣayyaadu assamak
Fisherman

نجّار
najjaar
Carpenter

رئيس
ra'iis
President

مدير
mudiir
Director

وزيرة
waziira
Minister

سفيرة
safiira
Ambassador

محامي
muḥaamii
Lawyer

قاضية
qaaḍiya
Judge

SPORTS AND GAMES

الرّياضة والألعاب

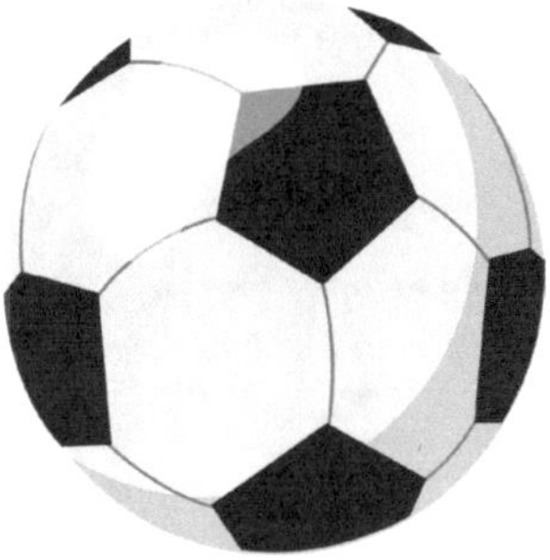

كرة
kura
Ball

الكرات
al kuraat
Marbles

لوح التزلّج
lawḥ attazalluj
Skateboard

التزلّج على الجليد
attazalluj ɛala al jaliid
Ice skating

لعبة ورق
luɛbatu waraq
Card game

لعبة الدّومينو
luɛbatu adduumiinuu
Domino game

كرة القدم
kuratu al qadam
Soccer US
Football GB

كرة اليد
kuratu al yadd
Handball

الكرة الطّائرة
al kura aṭṭaa'ira
Volleyball

كرة السّلّة
kuratu assalla
Basketball

سباحة
sibaaḥa
Swimming

سباق
sibaaq
Race

NUMBERS

الأرقام

صفر
ṣifr
Zero

واحد
waaḥid
One

اثنين
iṯnayn
Two

ثلاثة
ṯalaaṯa
Three

أربعة
arbaεa
Four

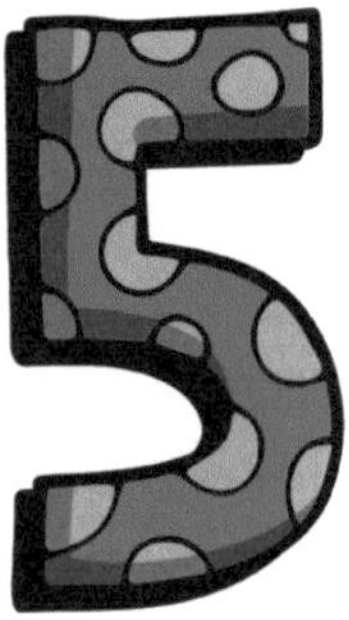

خمسة
xamsa
Five

ستّة
sitta
Six

سبعة
sabεa
Seven

ثمانية
ṯamaaniya
Eight

تسعة
tisεa
Nine

عشرة
εašara
Ten

أحد عشر
aḥada εašar
Eleven

12

اثنا عشر

iṯnaa ɛašar

Twelve

13

ثلاثة عشر

ṯalaaṯata ɛašar

Thirteen

14

أربعة عشر

arbaɛata ɛašar

Fourteen

15

خمسة عشر

xamsata ɛašar

Fifteen

16

ستّة عشر

sittata ɛašar

Sixteen

17

سبعة عشر

sabɛata ɛašar

Seventeen

18

ثمانية عشر
ṯamaaniyata εašar
Eighteen

19

تسعة عشر
tisεata εašar
Nineteen

20

عشرون
εišruun
Twenty

21

واحد و عشرون
waaḥid wa εišruun
Twenty-one

22

اثنان وعشرون
iṯnaani wa εišruun
Twenty-two

30

ثلاثون
ṯalaaṯuun
Thirty

40

أربعون
arbaɛuun
Forty

50

خمسون
xamsuun
Fifty

60

ستّون
sittuun
Sixty

70

سبعون
sabɛuun
Seventy

80

ثمانون
ṯamaanuun
Eighty

90

تسعون
tisɛuun
Ninety

100

مئة

mi'a

One hundred

110

مائة وعشرة

mi'a wa εašara

One hundred and ten

200

مائتان

mi'ataan

Two hundred

300

ثلاثمائة

t̲alaat̲umi'a

Three hundred

400

اربعمائة

arbaεumi'a

Four hundred

500

خمسمائة

xamsumi'a

Five hundred

600

ستّمائة
sittumi’a
Six hundred

700

سبعمائة
sabεumi’a
Seven hundred

800

ثمانمائة
ṯamaanumi’a
Eight hundred

900

تسعمائة
tisεumi’a
Nine hundred

1000

ألف
alf
One thousand

2000

ألفان
alfaan
Two thousand

GEOMETRIC SHAPES

الأشكال الهندسيّة

شعاع
šuεaaε
Radius

مَرْكَز
markaz
Center

زاوية
zaawiya
Angle

دائرة
daa’ira
Circle

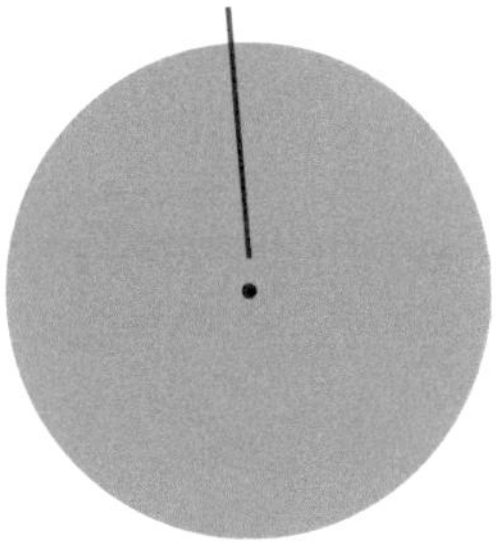

قرص
qurṣ
Disk / disc

مثلّث
mut̲allat̲
Triangle

مربّع
murabbaε
Square

مستطيل
mustaṭiil
Rectangle

مُعَيَّن
muεayyan
Rhombus

شبه منحرف
šibh munḥarif
Trapezium

إهليلج
ihliilij
Oval

خطّ
xaṭṭ
Line

COLORS

الألوان

أزرق
azraq
Blue

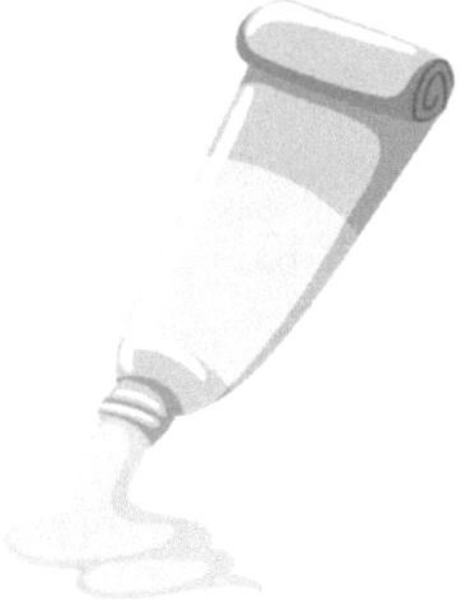

أصفر
aṣfar
Yellow

أسود
aswad
Black

أبيض
abyaḍ
White

أحمر
aḥmar
Red

أخضر
axḍar
Green

برتقالي
burtuqaalii
Orange

بنفسجي
banafsajii
Purple

بنّي
bunnii
Brown

وردي
wardii
Pink

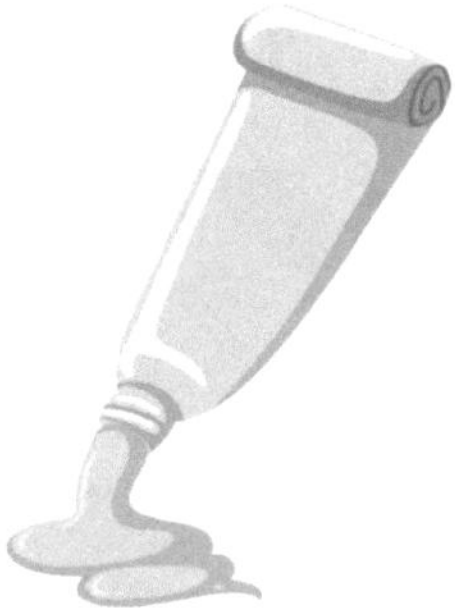

أخضر فاتح
axḍar faatiḥ
Light green

رمادي
ramaadii
Gray

EARTH

العالم، الأرض

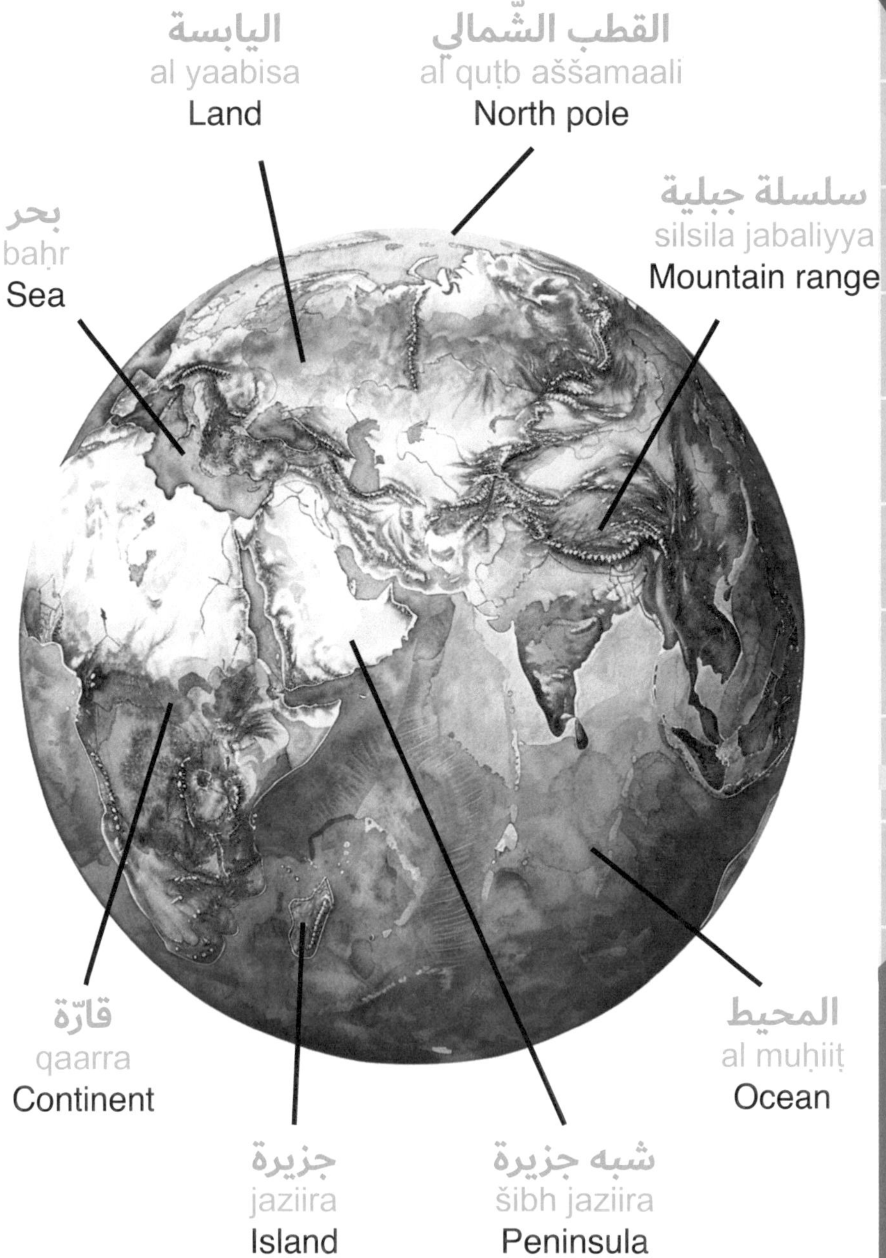
اليابسة
al yaabisa
Land
القطب الشّمالي
al quṭb aššamaali
North pole
بحر
baḥr
Sea
سلسلة جبلية
silsila jabaliyya
Mountain range
قارّة
qaarra
Continent
المحيط
al muḥiiṭ
Ocean
جزيرة
jaziira
Island
شبه جزيرة
šibh jaziira
Peninsula

TIME

الوقت

الأربعاء
al arbiεaa'
Wednesday

الخميس
al xamiis
Thursday

الجمعة
al jumuεa
Friday

الثّلاثاء
attulaataa'
Tuesday

السّبت
assabt
Saturday

الإثنين
al 'itnayn
Monday

السّنة
assana
Year

الأسبوع
al 'usbuuε
Week

الأحد
al aḥad
Sunday

الأمس
البارحة
al 'ams
al baariḥa
Yesterday

اليوم
al yawm
Today

غداً
ɣadan
Tomorrow

نهاية الأسبوع
nihaayat al 'usbuuε
Weekend

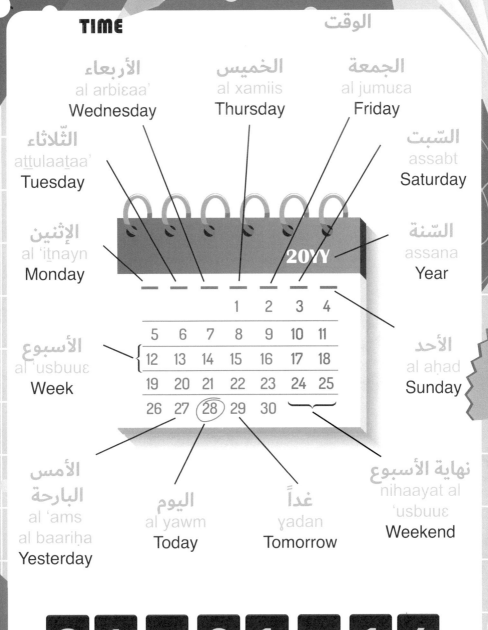

السّاعة
assaaεa
Hour

الدّقائق
addaqaa'iq
Minutes

الثّواني
attawaani
Seconds

MONTHS

الشّهور

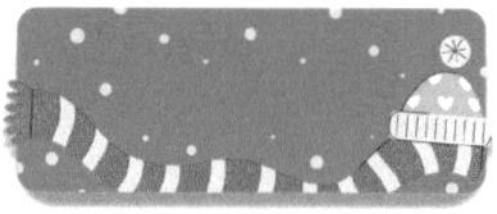

يناير
yanaayr
January

فبراير
fibraayr
February

مارس
maaris
March

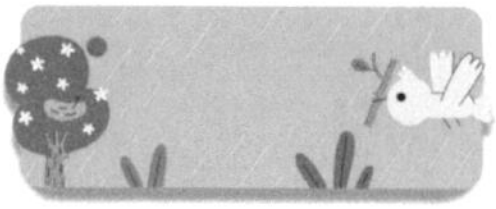

أبريل
abriil
April

مايو
maayuu
May

يونيو
yuunyuu
June

يوليوز
yuulyuuz
July

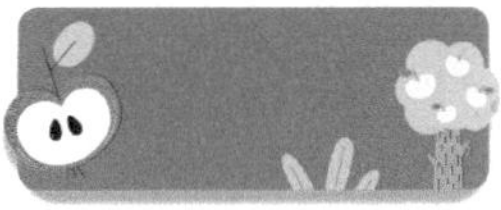

غشت
ɣušt
August

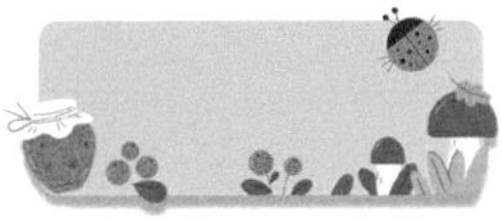

شتنبر
šutanbir
September

اكتوبر
uktuubar
October

نونبر
nuwanbir
November

دجنبر
dujanbir
December

Made in United States
Troutdale, OR
12/08/2024

26097032R00051